Thoughts From a Tornado - The Writings of a Chaotic Mind

AF624814

Rebecca L Drake

BookLeaf Publishing

Presentation by *BookLeaf Publishing*

Web: www.bookleafpub.com

E-mail: info@bookleafpub.com

ISBN: 9789357210744

First edition 2022

DEDICATION

Dedicated to everyone who ever believed in me. In particular my family, my partner, and my best friend.

PREFACE

I have written poetry since I was a teenager. It has always been something to ease my mind and get my swirling thoughts on paper. It eased my depression and helped my anxiety. I have long since figured out who I am as a person (mostly) and have found my voice as a writer. I hope you enjoy these thoughts from my tornado, the thoughts of a chaotic mind.

Itch

There's an itch inside my brain
Like a worm crawling around
Wearing me down
Eating me from the inside out
Try to stop it
Crying falling scratching
It gnaws at me growing in size
Sometimes I hold it back
slow it down
But mostly it consumes
Killing me daily
But I arise from the ashes
A Phoenix reborn
To try again day after day
Until the itch returns

Riptide

Caught in a riptide of despair
I can see the shore so close
The harder I struggle to get there
The farther away I am
Trapped by an undertow
Pulling me down
Down
Down
Deeper into the abyss
And all around me in the depths are my feelings
Some of them cling to me
Tiny parasites digging into my skin
Taking over my body
Living as I long to die
Others float by me just out of reach
Sometimes I catch one
Joy
Happiness
Reprieve
Until the current snatches them away
I can see the shoreline
The people I know standing there
Some trying to throw me a line but falling just
short
Others just watching as I drown

their words pushing me deeper
Down
Down
Farther into the abyss
Sometimes I remember what the shore feels like
The warmth of the sun on my face
The feel of the sand between my toes
The sweet salty smell of the sea air
Calling to me
But the current is too strong
The undertow too powerful
The parasites too intense
And so I drown
And as I sink I feel nothing
Because the parasites beneath my skin have
taken over
Slowly eroding away the tiny glimmers of hope
That I'll one day feel the sand beneath my feet
again
And I sink
Down
Down
Into the abyss
And the darkness swallows me
As the faint rays of sunlight up above slowly
fade
To nothing.

Lust

The soft caress of a man's hand on a woman's
hip.
He whispers the secrets of the world into her ear
As his hands set her body on fire.
The touch, taste, smell of sensuality
The erotic combination of sweat and sweet
words
Each holding the knowledge of the other's
desire.
The secret pleasures hidden in the folds of a
budding rose
Petals slowly opening, ripe with dew;
Waiting for the right moment, the right man
To discover them and make the rose bloom.

Sometimes

Sometimes life is roses, sweet words, gentle touches.
A text message sending love.
Soft whispers in a night of tangled limbs.

Sometimes life is passion, intensity, fervent desire.
Subtle innuendo, grasping at skin.
The desperation of two lovers full of need.

Sometimes life is excitement, full of newness and wonder.
Trying new things, places unknown.
Reveling in the wonder of experience.

Sometimes life is ordinary, going through the motions.
Laundry getting done, waking with our children.
The simple pleasure of a family meal.

Sometimes life is chaos, a whirlwind of emotion.
Arguments ensuing, a buildup of stress.
Working together to get through to the end.

Sometimes life is understanding, patience and knowledge.
Knowing your partner needs space or time.
Or maybe a gentle touch of redirection or support.

Sometimes life is pain, suffering and desperation.
Getting caught up in the darkness that overwhelms.
Struggling to climb our way out, together.

Sometimes life is hopelessness, fearing the unknown.
Not knowing what to do, feeling you are drowning.
Holding onto the person you love, trying to get by.

These are the lives I want to share with you.

Fly Away

Doors slam
Footsteps on the stairs,

You leave
Tears streaming down your face.

Mom cries
Her heart torn open at the seams.

She looks
Her little bird is gone.

Fly away
You little fleeing bird.

Wings spread,
Why did you go so far?

You return
Things happen slowly like before.

Then fast,
The argument crescendos.

You fly,
Leaving me once again

For good,
I know you won't return.

Fly away
Precious little bird.

Go slowly
I want to fly with you.

Ocean

As the sun arises and the day begins anew,
I sit upon a silent beach and wonder what you'd do,

If you were sitting on the beach right by my side,
Looking at the ocean and smiling at the tide.

The sky is shades of pink, red and yellow too;
And the vast expanse of ocean is a variety of blue.

As I sit on my towel and wonder what you'd say,
The ocean reaches near with fingers cold as clay.

When I dream of you and I sharing what we feel,
My dream begins, quite suddenly, to seem very real.

The sun shines down upon us casting shadows in the sand,
And in my dream, romantically, you offer me your hand.

You gently pull me to my feet and silently you walk,
Together gazing at the sky, neither of us talk.

And as we continue walking along the never-ending sand,
Night descends upon us and covers up the land.

The sea is very dark now and the moon presents a glow,
Radiant and beautiful upon all I know.

Even in the darkness when we can't see the sand,
You guide me safely on with the softness of your hand.

Then suddenly you stop and stare at the dark expanse of blue,
You tell me that you love me and I don't know what to do.

For the longest time I’ve waited for you to say those simple words,
That make my heart soar like a million tiny birds.

With all my heart I love you, I know that will always be,

The love that courses through my veins is
greater than the sea.

As my dream begins to fade and you start to go
away,
I wonder in my heart if there will be another day,

When we will walk and talk and have a lot of
fun
On a beach made out of love and dreams that
have begun.

See your love is like the ocean and the beach is
like your heart,
It has the greatness of the sea, but the sand is
where it starts.

Man on the Moon

Last night I dreamt of the man on the moon,
He came to me in an inky-dark dream.
We danced a waltz to a music-less tune,
With promises made by a silent stream.
The darkened Eve was split by his sweet light,
We moved gracefully to our quiet song,
Strangers brought together in dreams at night.
Our hearts combine as one where they belong.
Each so alone and yet together whole,
Filling a void made empty by lost love.
As we complete the other's lost soul,
Till at last he returns to his home above.
He still comes to dance my loneliness away,
Better feet, than heart, ache in the light of day.

Eternity in a Grain of Sand

I love the feeling of the sand between my toes.
Soft breeze tugging gently at my hair.
The smell of the warm, salt sea filling the air.
Quietly seeking and tickling my nose.

I love the sweet sound the ocean makes.
The music of water flowing at me.
The boiling surge of saline sea.
The symphonic song as each wave breaks.

I love the everlasting meeting of ocean and sky.
Forever merging into the horizon.
The sea that moves eternally on.
Timeless, salty deep, unending to my naked eye.

I love the life that surges in the depth of the sea.
An enigma, another universe.
A wealth of life, exceedingly diverse.
A world of its own; huge, unending, free.

I love the ocean - it holds existence in the palm of its hand.
The emergence of life so sublime -
The undying ebb and flow of time -
The sea embraces eternity in a grain of sand.

Trampoline

Twang, Twoing, Boing.
Twang, Twoing, Boing.
Up and down, down and up.
"Come on the trampoline."
She calls me to join her.
Twang, Twoing, Boing.
The springs protest her rapid-fire jumping.
It would be fun to jump with her.
Flying through the air.
It is like a rush.
The blood flows through your body.
I join her because I will be leaving.
Maybe.
Do I have to grow up?
Do I have to stop jumping on the trampoline?
When we put the trampoline together she wouldn't get off.
Such a project getting each spring in place.
It would fall apart otherwise.
I want to keep jumping now,
As she jumped forever that first day.
I am weightless as I jump. I am free from my inner thoughts.
Then my feet slip out from under me.

I am weightless for a moment more,
Then I crash to the canvas of the trampoline.
The springs groan as I fall.
And then it is still.
I wish I could jump forever.
I have to go.
Twang, Twoing, Boing.
The sound follows me as I leave.

Do You

Do you think before you speak?
Your voice is full of scorn.
Acid dripping from your words
As they tumble from your mouth.

Do you care whose heart you break?
Your words inflicting pain.
The sting of thorns that pierce and probe
Berating, mocking thoughts.

Do you think that I believe
Your shallow, cold regret?
Empty words of meaningless sludge
Falling from your lips too late.

“A”

Upended youth
Due to childish whims
Think not, thought not
Of repercussions
Not tears of joy
But rather pain
You'll never be
A child again
Drip drop drip drop
A childhood gone
Flip flop flip flop
What must be done
Lost youth grows weary
Old too soon
Sighs of regret
As pregnancy looms.

Mind Over Me

Keeping my mind occupied
By the thoughts inside
Swirling in my head
Trying to hide

Stressed to the max, too much to do
The day's never through
I try to sleep instead
To hide what's true

Few people know the turmoil I feel
A fear that's too real
Of dreams gone dead
And the hope fear steals

Living a life swimming through the muck
In a life that is stuck
My heart has been bled
There is no luck

I question myself, who should I be
Is this really me
This life that I've led
I don't feel free

But then I step back and look at things I have done
At memories of fun
I put fear to bed
I know I've won

Headache

There's a headache deep within my brain
Bubbles to the daylight, stops
Penetrating eyes and skull
Staying, staying, growing stronger
Lasting longer
Stress and pain, it comes again
I beg it, will it, curse it gone
And slowly, hesitating
As if it is still waiting
For more pain, more fear, more tears
It goes, lingering
For one last moment
Looking back
Faintly reminding
Dulling eyes and heart
Until it's gone
The fear, the pain, the stress remain
To provoke the ache within my brain

So Different Yet I Love You Still

We walk a mile in shoes that don't match
Wondering why our feet hurt
Yet ignoring the blisters
We walk a mile in shoes that don't fit
And we wonder why they fall off
Or squeeze too tightly
We loved them in the store
Seemed so perfect
Shiny and new
When we walked our first mile
The shoes lost their shine
But we kept them still
Then came a second mile and a third
And each time it got harder
As the shoes loosened or pinched
But we loved them still
After the fourth and fifth
The miles were longer
The pain more acute
Then they began to fall apart
Too much for a mismatched pair
That didn't fit in the first place
But we wanted them still
So we taped and patched

We tried to be gentle
And then they were gone
We walked until the miles were too much
Yet we long for them still

Rain

Tears run down my face
Tiny drops of rain
As I struggle with my brain
And the pain within it.

The clouds grow dark
Rumbling as the pain grows
And what nobody knows
Is that it never abates.

Every day it changes
Sometimes the sky weeps
Except when my brain sleeps
And then the pain stops.

Until it comes back stronger
My constant friend
Will it ever end
Or will the rain never release me?

Loneliness

Loneliness washes over her
Like leaves in the wind
She is overtaken
Tossed aside
Blown away

He came to her in the night
That's how it began
Sweet sleepless nights
Heavy breaths
Tired limbs

She knew she wasn't the only one
He was only hers at night
When the wind howled
And the dogs bayed at the moon
He was with her

Then one day it was over
Like the flash of a bulb it was done
Where there was darkness
There was nothing
But the bitter loneliness

Spring

Today the sun shines down upon me
The warm rays on my face
Radiating joy and content

I feel the warmth of a spring breeze
Sweeping through my hair
Tickling my skin

The sweet smell of grass and lilac
Gently caressing my nose
And assaulting my senses

For My Babies

The day I found out about you
Was the day my life began
Tick tock went the clock
As I waited for you to grow
Tiny hands and tiny feet
Perfection
The day you were born
Was the day my life changed
Little button nose
Sleepy eyes drawn to mine
A love incomparable
Every day you grow
Is a day full of wonder
First walking and talking
Then so much more
Soon enough you'll be older
And you'll learn how to fly
And I will be proud of you
My beautiful babies

Black and Blue

I try to hide the pains inside
Behind bulky sweaters and warm pants
They are hidden deep down
Only I can see them
Inky dark black and blue
Permeating my skin
Like painful, ugly tattoos
"But I love you," he says
As his hands inflict pain
"Forgive me," he pleads
As the colors bloom beneath my skin
And then it happens again
And again
And again
Until one day
He goes too far
Hands on my throat
Bruises on my skin
Pain in my heart
And I explode
White hot heat boiling forth
"Enough," I whisper
"Enough," I scream
And then the world turns black
"I'm sorry"
"I love you"

Somewhere

Somewhere over the Rainbow
Lies the hidden secrets of my soul
The wants
The needs
The desires
I long for the gentle caress of the night breeze
against my naked skin
My heart beating rhythmically beneath your
hands
As they slide along my back
Warmth pooling as I wait for your touch
Somewhere over the Rainbow
Lies my deepest desires
Gentle touch and not so gentle caresses
As you tug my hair
and tell me that you love me
Again
And again
Somewhere over the Rainbow
Lies the relief that I hope for
Like the winding of a clock
Too tight with springs ready to burst
The pressure building
Until it breaks free
And it washes over me
Somewhere over the Rainbow

Sleep

It's dark
I'm tired but I can't sleep
I'm not sure why really
I just can't.
When I can't sleep I like to dream
No not dream, really
But imagine, in my mind, like a dream.
Tales of love and adventure
A soothing balm
To a chaotic mind.

www.ingramcontent.com/pod-product-compliance
Lightning Source LLC
Chambersburg PA
CBHW051753130826
49812CB00033B/1128
* 9 7 8 9 3 5 7 2 1 0 7 4 4 *